GARY CHAPMAN
RAMON PRESSO

Love Talks

FOR COUPLES

101 Questions to Stimulate Interaction with Your Spouse

NORTHFIELD PUBLISHING
CHICAGO

Two entries (#37,#54) first appeared in Ramon Presson, *Soul Care* (Littleton, Colo.: Serendipity House, 2000).

ISBN: 1-881273-48-2

3 5 7 9 10 8 6 4 2

Printed in the United States of America

Tips for Using Love Talks

Your spouse is a fascinating person, a treasure trove of meaningful, humorous, and profound experiences, thoughts, feelings, ideas, memories, hopes, dreams, beliefs, and convictions. These questions celebrate the depth and wonderful mystery of your mate. Questions invite disclosure, and disclosure launches discovery. Discovery enriches a marriage and builds intimacy. Use the following 101 questions to prompt meaningful, in-depth discussions and to affirm and encourage your spouse.

Here are some ways to use the questions:

- During dinner at home (if you don't have children)
- During a quiet moment in the evening
- At bedtime (if both of you are alert)
- During dinner on a date night
- While in the car during a long drive

While the easiest way to proceed through the questions is to use them in the order they are presented, another possibility is that your spouse and you take turns in selecting the questions. We recommend that you do only one or two questions at a time. These questions are like dessert—a small and satisfying portion creates the anticipation for more later. *Love Talks* offers a process to enjoy, not a project to complete.

Have fun with these questions two or three times each week and watch intimacy grow in your marriage.

*What are two things that happened today,
and how did you feel about them?*

Love Talks
FOR COUPLES

— QUESTION 1 —

What are two things that happened today,

and how did you feel about them?

Love Talks

FOR COUPLES

— QUESTION 2 —

What were some of your favorite toys as a child?

What was your favorite candy?

What were some of your favorite toys as a child?

What was your favorite candy?

Love Talks

FOR COUPLES

*Describe the home of one or both sets
of your grandparents.*

— QUESTION 3 —

Describe the home of one or both sets

of your grandparents.

Love Talks

FOR COUPLES

— QUESTION 4 —

What was something you really wanted but were not allowed to own as a child or teen?

Love Talks
FOR COUPLES

— QUESTION 4 —

What was something you really wanted but were not allowed to own as a child or teen?

Love Talks
FOR COUPLES

— QUESTION 5 —

*Describe one of your favorite
elementary school teachers. Then describe a favorite*

☐ *high school teacher*

☐ *college professor*

Love Talks
FOR COUPLES

Describe one of your favorite

elementary school teachers. Then describe a favorite

☐ *high school teacher*

☐ *college professor*

As you were growing up, what was unique about your family as compared to other families in your neighborhood or the families of your friends?

Love Talks
FOR COUPLES

As you were growing up, what was unique about your family as compared to other families in your neighborhood or the families of your friends?

Love Talks
FOR COUPLES

What was your most serious physical injury

as a child or teen?

What was your most serious physical injury

as a child or teen?

What do you remember about learning to drive?

What do you remember about learning to drive?

Can you recall visiting your parent's workplace?

If so, describe it and how you felt when you went there.

Love Talks
FOR COUPLES

Can you recall visiting your parent's workplace?
If so, describe it and how you felt when you went there.

Complete this sentence:

"I'm sure my mom and dad wish I would . . . ."

Love Talks
FOR COUPLES

*C*omplete this sentence:

"I'm sure my mom and dad wish I would . . . ."

*L*ove *T*alks

FOR COUPLES

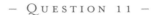

— QUESTION 11 —

What is perhaps the worst movie you have ever seen?

Love Talks

FOR COUPLES

What is perhaps the worst movie you have ever seen?

Love Talks

FOR COUPLES

– QUESTION 12 –

What tragic news story in the last few years

made you particularly sad?

Love Talks
FOR COUPLES

What tragic news story in the last few years

made you particularly sad?

— QUESTION 13 —

What was one of the most memorable weddings (other than your own) that you have attended?

Love Talks
FOR COUPLES

*W*hat was one of the most memorable weddings
(other than your own) that you have attended?

*L*ove *T*alks
FOR COUPLES

— QUESTION 14 —

What is something you collected as a child or teen?

— QUESTION 14 —

What is something you collected as a child or teen?

Love Talks

FOR COUPLES

— QUESTION 15 —

*What is a question that you wish you had the courage
to ask your mother and/or father?*

Love Talks
FOR COUPLES

What is a question that you wish you had the courage to ask your mother and/or father?

Love Talks
FOR COUPLES

If you were given five acres of land, where would

you want it to be and what would you want to do with it?

Love Talks

FOR COUPLES

If you were given five acres of land, where would you want it to be and what would you want to do with it?

*If you could own and operate your own business
(and be guaranteed of its success), what would it be?*

Love Talks
FOR COUPLES

*If you could own and operate your own business
(and be guaranteed of its success), what would it be?*

If you do not play a musical instrument,
what one do you wish you could play?
If you do/did play a musical instrument, do you
recall how you chose that particular one?

Love Talks
FOR COUPLES

*If you do not play a musical instrument,
what one do you wish you could play?
If you do/did play a musical instrument, do you
recall how you chose that particular one?*

What would you say are two of the best concerts

you have seen, either in person or on television?

Love Talks

FOR COUPLES

— QUESTION 19 —

What would you say are two of the best concerts you have seen, either in person or on television?

Love Talks
FOR COUPLES

*What are two of your all-time
favorite movies (or books)?*

What are two of your all-time favorite movies (or books)?

Love Talks
FOR COUPLES

My mother/father clearly did not understand what was considered cool when she/he bought me . . .

Love Talks

FOR COUPLES

— QUESTION 21 —

My mother/father clearly did not understand what was considered cool when she/he bought me . . .

Love Talks
FOR COUPLES

What famous person (deceased)

would you like to have met?

Love Talks

FOR COUPLES

What famous person (deceased)

would you like to have met?

Which of the following would you find most gratifying?

☐ *earning a Ph.D.*

☐ *publishing a best-selling book*

☐ *recording an original chart-topping song*

☐ *winning an Olympic gold medal*

Love Talks
FOR COUPLES

Which of the following would you find most gratifying?

☐ *earning a Ph.D.*

☐ *publishing a best-selling book*

☐ *recording an original chart-topping song*

☐ *winning an Olympic gold medal*

Love Talks
FOR COUPLES

— QUESTION 24 —

*If money and/or childcare were no object,
what would be your idea of the perfect New Year's Eve?*

Love Talks
FOR COUPLES

*If money and/or childcare were no object,
what would be your idea of the perfect New Year's Eve?*

Love Talks
FOR COUPLES

Who is one of the most genuinely spiritual persons you know?

Love Talks
FOR COUPLES

Who is one of the most genuinely

spiritual persons you know?

Love Talks
FOR COUPLES

*O*ne writer referred to the day before

the horrific events of September 11, 2001

as *"The World As We Knew It."*

In your opinion, how is the world different?

How has that episode changed your thinking in some way?

*L*ove *T*alks

FOR COUPLES

*O*ne writer referred to the day before

the horrific events of September 11, 2001

as *"The World As We Knew It."*

In your opinion, how is the world different?

How has that episode changed your thinking in some way?

Which of the following rides would be your first choice?

☐ a gondola in Venice   ☐ an airboat in the Everglades

☐ a cab in London   ☐ a raft down the Colorado River

☐ a Ferrari on the Autobahn   ☐ a carriage in Paris

☐ a hot air balloon in Switzerland

Love Talks
FOR COUPLES

Which of the following rides would be your first choice?

☐ a gondola in Venice   ☐ an airboat in the Everglades

☐ a cab in London   ☐ a raft down the Colorado River

☐ a Ferrari on the Autobahn   ☐ a carriage in Paris

☐ a hot air balloon in Switzerland

Love Talks

FOR COUPLES

What is one of your favorite memories

that includes snow?

What is one of your favorite memories that includes snow?

Love Talks
FOR COUPLES

Who was your favorite superhero or cartoon character?

Who was your favorite superhero or cartoon character?

If someone could bless you and pass on to you a special ability, whom would you choose to bless you and with what ability?

Love Talks
FOR COUPLES

*If someone could bless you and pass on to you
a special ability, whom would you choose
to bless you and with what ability?*

— QUESTION 31 —

Who is the most joyful person you know?

Who is the most joyful person you know?

Who is someone whom you wish you could

infect with a more positive attitude?

Love Talks

FOR COUPLES

Who is someone whom you wish you could

infect with a more positive attitude?

– QUESTION 33 –

*C*omplete this sentence:

"It would make me a better person if I

were more like you in the way you . . . ."

Complete this sentence:

"It would make me a better person if I

were more like you in the way you . . . ."

Love Talks

FOR COUPLES

When in your life would you say your

self-esteem was the lowest?

Love Talks
FOR COUPLES

When in your life would you say your self-esteem was the lowest?

Love Talks
FOR COUPLES

Recall a time when you were given constructive criticism that proved beneficial.

Love Talks
FOR COUPLES

Recall a time when you were given constructive criticism that proved beneficial.

Love Talks
FOR COUPLES

$\mathcal{T}$he lion, otter, beaver, and golden retriever

are used to describe four personality types.

Which one do you think best describes you?

☐ Lion—strong, confident, leader, likes to make sure things get done

☐ Otter—very outgoing, enjoys people, humorous, creative

☐ Beaver—detail oriented, organized, follows instructions, good with projects

☐ Golden Retriever—loyal, sensitive, encouraging

$\mathcal{L}$ove $\mathcal{T}$alks
FOR COUPLES

The lion, otter, beaver, and golden retriever

are used to describe four personality types.

Which one do you think best describes you?

☐ Lion—strong, confident, leader,
likes to make sure things get done

☐ Otter—very outgoing, enjoys people,
humorous, creative

☐ Beaver—detail oriented, organized,
follows instructions, good with
projects

☐ Golden Retriever—loyal, sensitive,
encouraging

— QUESTION 37 —

*If you could hire Martha Stewart for a day,
what would you have her do?*

Love Talks
FOR COUPLES

If you could hire Martha Stewart for a day,

what would you have her do?

Love Talks

FOR COUPLES

Regardless of how long I live,

I hope I will always . . . .

Love Talks
FOR COUPLES

Regardless of how long I live,

I hope I will always . . . .

Love Talks
FOR COUPLES

— QUESTION 39 —

"It is more blessed to give than to receive."
Recall a gift that gave you considerable
satisfaction in presenting it.

Love Talks
FOR COUPLES

"It is more blessed to give than to receive."
Recall a gift that gave you considerable
satisfaction in presenting it.

Describe the location and three features

of your dream home.

Love Talks

FOR COUPLES

Describe the location and three features

of your dream home.

Love Talks

FOR COUPLES

— QUESTION 41 —

From whom would you most like

to hear one of the following?

☐ *"I love you."*   ☐ *"I appreciate you."*

☐ *"I support you."*   ☐ *"I miss you."*

☐ *"I respect you."*   ☐ *"I trust you."*

Love Talks
FOR COUPLES

From whom would you most like

to hear one of the following?

☐ *"I love you."*   ☐ *"I appreciate you."*

☐ *"I support you."*   ☐ *"I miss you."*

☐ *"I respect you."*   ☐ *"I trust you."*

In retrospect, what is something that your parents

were wise in doing in raising you?

In retrospect, what is something that your parents were wise in doing in raising you?

Love Talks
FOR COUPLES

What was your most/least favorite subject in school?

What was your most/least favorite subject in school?

If you could take a course in any subject right now
at your local college, what type of course would it be?

If you could take a course in any subject right now at your local college, what type of course would it be?

Love Talks
FOR COUPLES

In what way are you most/least like your mother?

How are you most/least like your father?

— QUESTION 45 —

In what way are you most/least like your mother?

How are you most/least like your father?

Love Talks
FOR COUPLES

In Matthew 6:34, Jesus encourages us to live with faith

in the present. Which is the greater obstacle for you?

☐ *rehearsing the past*

☐ *worrying about the future*

— QUESTION 46 —

In Matthew 6:34, Jesus encourages us to live with faith

in the present. Which is the greater obstacle for you?

☐ *rehearsing the past*

☐ *worrying about the future*

— QUESTION 47 —

Who was your best friend in junior high school?

What did you do together?

Love Talks

FOR COUPLES

Who was your best friend in junior high school?

What did you do together?

— QUESTION 48 —

As I was growing up, my father was most like

☐ a coach   ☐ a preacher

☐ a judge   ☐ a manager

☐ an historian   ☐ a cheerleader

☐ a professor   ☐ other

Love Talks
FOR COUPLES

As I was growing up, my father was most like

☐ *a coach* ☐ *a preacher*

☐ *a judge* ☐ *a manager*

☐ *an historian* ☐ *a cheerleader*

☐ *a professor* ☐ *other*

Love Talks
FOR COUPLES

If you inherited $200,000 (after taxes),

what would you do with the money?

Love Talks
FOR COUPLES

If you inherited $200,000 (after taxes),

what would you do with the money?

Love Talks

FOR COUPLES

— QUESTION 50 —

Name three jobs or careers

you are definitely not suited for.

Love Talks

FOR COUPLES

— QUESTION 50 —

*Name three jobs or careers
you are definitely not suited for.*

Describe your pediatrician when you were growing up.

What do you remember about those doctor visits?

— QUESTION 51 —

Describe your pediatrician when you were growing up.

What do you remember about those doctor visits?

— QUESTION 52 —

Concerning what biblical topic or Bible passage (or verse) do you wish you had a better understanding?

Love Talks

FOR COUPLES

Concerning what biblical topic or Bible passage (or verse)
do you wish you had a better understanding?

What do you think that you will want to do

in your retirement years?

Love Talks
FOR COUPLES

What do you think that you will want to do

in your retirement years?

Love Talks

FOR COUPLES

Acts 2:42-47 describes a close, caring community.
In what setting have you had the greatest
experience of genuine fellowship?

☐ *friends at school*   ☐ *job where I worked*   ☐ *sports team*

☐ *support group*   ☐ *church-related group*   ☐ *volunteer organization*

☐ *ministry/mission team*   ☐ *fraternity/sorority*   ☐ *other* _____

Love Talks
FOR COUPLES

*A*cts 2:42–47 describes a close, caring community.
In what setting have you had the greatest
experience of genuine fellowship?

☐ friends at school ☐ job where I worked ☐ sports team

☐ support group ☐ church-related group ☐ volunteer organization

☐ ministry/mission team ☐ fraternity/sorority ☐ other _____

Love Talks
FOR COUPLES

— QUESTION 55 —

What item of clothing in my wardrobe

do you really like to see me wear?

Love Talks
FOR COUPLES

What item of clothing in my wardrobe

do you really like to see me wear?

Love Talks
FOR COUPLES

What is a song or piece of music

that moves or inspires you?

*W*hat is a song or piece of music

that moves or inspires you?

*L*ove *T*alks
FOR COUPLES

What quality or skill that you possess would you find most gratifying to have your child imitate as an adult?

Love Talks
FOR COUPLES

What quality or skill that you possess would you find most gratifying to have your child imitate as an adult?

If you could win any competition in the world,

what would it be?

Love Talks
FOR COUPLES

If you could win any competition in the world,

what would it be?

Love Talks

FOR COUPLES

What nonbiblical historical event

would you like to have witnessed?

— QUESTION 59 —

What nonbiblical historical event

would you like to have witnessed?

Love Talks
FOR COUPLES

Name the Old Testament event that you wish you could have witnessed. Name the New Testament event (in addition to the Resurrection) that you wish you could have witnessed.

Name the Old Testament event that you wish you could have witnessed. Name the New Testament event (in addition to the Resurrection) that you wish you could have witnessed.

Love Talks
FOR COUPLES

In TV's The Andy Griffith Show, *Barney Fife once told*
Andy that the biggest purchase he ever made was
a septic tank for his parents' wedding anniversary.
What gift would you like to give to your parents?

In TV's The Andy Griffith Show, *Barney Fife once told
Andy that the biggest purchase he ever made was
a septic tank for his parents' wedding anniversary.
What gift would you like to give to your parents?*

Love Talks
FOR COUPLES

What is something you thoroughly enjoyed doing

as a child and have not done in years?

What is something you thoroughly enjoyed doing

as a child and have not done in years?

Richard Foster insists that our lives are bombarded by hurry, crowds, and noise. Which of those three has been most bothersome for you lately?

Love Talks

FOR COUPLES

*R*ichard Foster insists that our lives are bombarded
by hurry, crowds, and noise. Which of those three
has been most bothersome for you lately?

Love Talks
FOR COUPLES

*C*omplete this sentence: *"A time that I felt I might*

be in physical danger was when . . ."

Love Talks

FOR COUPLES

Complete this sentence: "A time that I felt I might be in physical danger was when . . ."

In what event would you most like to win an Olympic gold medal?

In what event would you most like

to win an Olympic gold medal?

Love Talks
FOR COUPLES

Recall a time when you were disappointed

in not being chosen.

Love Talks
FOR COUPLES

Recall a time when you were disappointed

in not being chosen.

Love Talks

FOR COUPLES

— QUESTION 67 —

I wish I could hire _____ to write and record

a song from me to you.

I wish I could hire _____ to write and record

a song from me to you.

Love Talks
FOR COUPLES

I think I would crack under the torture if I were forced

to listen to only _____ music all day and

could only eat _____ meals all day.

— QUESTION 68 —

I think I would crack under the torture if I were forced

to listen to only _____ music all day and

could only eat _____ meals all day.

Love Talks

FOR COUPLES

If we were to adopt a child from another country,

which country would it be?

If we were to adopt a child from another country,

which country would it be?

As a couple we make a great team, but it is

most unlikely that we would ever team up to. . .

- [ ] *win a mixed-doubles tennis championship*
- [ ] *sing a duet*
- [ ] *win a medal in couples figure skating*
- [ ] *be co-leaders (main speakers) of a nationally televised marriage seminar*

- [ ] *compete in a ballroom dancing competition*
- [ ] *operate a Bed & Breakfast Inn*
- [ ] *co-author a book entitled "Stress-Free Parenting"*

Love Talks

FOR COUPLES

As a couple we make a great team, but it is

most unlikely that we would ever team up to. . .

- [ ] win a mixed-doubles tennis championship
- [ ] sing a duet
- [ ] win a medal in couples figure skating
- [ ] be co-leaders (main speakers) of a nationally televised marriage seminar

- [ ] compete in a ballroom dancing competition
- [ ] operate a Bed & Breakfast Inn
- [ ] co-author a book entitled "Stress-Free Parenting"

Love Talks
FOR COUPLES

— QUESTION 71 —

Imagine that your internal dashboard has a spiritual

passion gauge on it. What is your present reading?

E ____

¼ ____

½ ____

¾ ____

F ____

Imagine that your internal dashboard has a spiritual passion gauge on it. What is your present reading?

E ____

¼ ____

½ ____

¾ ____

F ____

Love Talks
FOR COUPLES

— QUESTION 72 —

What is the worst or most unusual

job interview you ever had?

Love Talks

FOR COUPLES

What is the worst or most unusual

job interview you ever had?

Love Talks

FOR COUPLES

The circus act that most reminds me of my job is . . .

The circus act that most reminds me of my job is . . .

What is your most/least favorite trait in others?

Love Talks
FOR COUPLES

— QUESTION 74 —

What is your most/least favorite trait in others?

What kind of race best describes your last seven days?

BOSTON MARATHON
It seemed to last forever

TOUR DE FRANCE
I was peddling uphill as fast as I could

KENTUCKY DERBY
*I worked for so long on something
that was over so quickly*

INDIANAPOLIS 500
*I went round and round,
and I'm right where I started*

IRONMAN TRIATHLON
*I endured a week full of job,
family, and church activities*

24 HOURS OF LE MANS
Sleep? What's that?

HUNDRED-METER HIGH HURDLES
All I did was sprint and navigate obstacles

DEMOLITION DERBY
I feel beat up

What kind of race best describes your last seven days?

BOSTON MARATHON
It seemed to last forever

TOUR DE FRANCE
I was peddling uphill as fast as I could

KENTUCKY DERBY
*I worked for so long on something
that was over so quickly*

INDIANAPOLIS 500
*I went round and round,
and I'm right where I started*

IRONMAN TRIATHLON
*I endured a week full of job,
family, and church activities*

24 HOURS OF LE MANS
Sleep? What's that?

HUNDRED-METER HIGH HURDLES
All I did was sprint and navigate obstacles

DEMOLITION DERBY
I feel beat up

Love Talks
FOR COUPLES

Talk about your early experiences with someone of another race or nationality.

Love Talks

FOR COUPLES

— QUESTION 76 —

Talk about your early experiences with someone of another race or nationality.

Love Talks
FOR COUPLES

Describe a summer camp experience.

Describe a summer camp experience.

Love Talks
FOR COUPLES

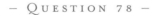

— QUESTION 78 —

What is your favorite Disney animated film?

Love Talks

FOR COUPLES

What is your favorite Disney animated film?

— QUESTION 79 —

When you were growing up,
where did your family go on vacations?
Describe one of those vacations.

Love Talks
FOR COUPLES

*When you were growing up,
where did your family go on vacations?
Describe one of those vacations.*

Can you remember a time when you got lost or separated from your family or companions? Describe what happened and how you felt.

Love Talks
FOR COUPLES

— QUESTION 80 —

*C*an you remember a time when you got lost
or separated from your family or companions?
Describe what happened and how you felt.

Love Talks

FOR COUPLES

Recall a time when you got sick

at a very inopportune time.

*Recall a time when you got sick
at a very inopportune time.*

Love Talks

FOR COUPLES

What high school or college course would you rather flee the country than be forced to take again?

What high school or college course would you rather flee the country than be forced to take again?

Love Talks
FOR COUPLES

Can you recall a first date during which you immediately knew there would not be a second date?

Love Talks

FOR COUPLES

Can you recall a first date during which you immediately knew there would not be a second date?

*Select and describe a couple who were friends
with your parents when you were growing up.*

Select and describe a couple who were friends

with your parents when you were growing up.

— QUESTION 85 —

Recall a childhood memory about one of the following:

☐ *playing in a creek* ☐ *pretending to be a superhero*

☐ *playing in a treehouse* ☐ *a slumber party or sleepover*

☐ *catching fireflies* ☐ *jumping off the high dive*

☐ *running a lemonade stand*

Recall a childhood memory about one of the following:

- [ ] *playing in a creek*
- [ ] *playing in a treehouse*
- [ ] *catching fireflies*
- [ ] *running a lemonade stand*

- [ ] *pretending to be a superhero*
- [ ] *a slumber party or sleepover*
- [ ] *jumping off the high dive*

Love Talks
FOR COUPLES

escribe your parents' reaction on the day

you moved out or left for college.

Describe your parents' reaction on the day

you moved out or left for college.

Recall something special about your high school

or college graduation.

Recall something special about your high school or college graduation.

Love Talks

FOR COUPLES

— QUESTION 88 —

What is your favorite scene from your favorite movie?

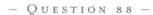

What is your favorite scene from your favorite movie?

I thought it was one of the coolest items in my wardrobe at the time, but today I'm not sure I'd even wear it to a costume party. What is it?

I thought it was one of the coolest items in my wardrobe at the time, but today I'm not sure I'd even wear it to a costume party. What is it?

Love Talks
FOR COUPLES

*S*omething I wanted to quit

but my parents wouldn't let me was . . .

Something I wanted to quit

but my parents wouldn't let me was . . .

Love Talks

FOR COUPLES

Joseph's brothers sold him into slavery. If you have siblings, what was one of the meanest things done to you by a brother or sister? If you are an only child, what was one of the meanest things done to you by a friend?

Love Talks
FOR COUPLES

Joseph's brothers sold him into slavery. If you have siblings, what was one of the meanest things done to you by a brother or sister? If you are an only child, what was one of the meanest things done to you by a friend?

— QUESTION 92 —

Describe someone you encountered recently who probably needs God in his or her life.

Love Talks
FOR COUPLES

Describe someone you encountered recently who probably needs God in his or her life.

Love Talks
FOR COUPLES

If you were offered the opportunity to be one of the contestants on Survivor, *would you do it? If yes, what do you imagine would be the hardest thing for you to cope with?*

Love Talks

FOR COUPLES

If you were offered the opportunity to be one of the contestants on Survivor, *would you do it? If yes, what do you imagine would be the hardest thing for you to cope with?*

One of the descendants of King Saul was named Mephibosheth. Do you like your first name? If you could choose another first name for yourself, what would it be?

Love Talks
FOR COUPLES

One of the descendants of King Saul was named Mephibosheth. Do you like your first name? If you could choose another first name for yourself, what would it be?

In the movie The Karate Kid, *young Daniel is befriended by an old Japanese man who teaches him karate, but more importantly offers him kindness and encouragement. Name an older person who blessed you with kindness and encouragement.*

Love Talks
FOR COUPLES

In the movie The Karate Kid, *young Daniel is befriended by an old Japanese man who teaches him karate, but more importantly offers him kindness and encouragement. Name an older person who blessed you with kindness and encouragement.*

Love Talks
FOR COUPLES

What is one of your favorite stories that

your parents tell about you?

Love Talks

FOR COUPLES

What is one of your favorite stories that

your parents tell about you?

Love Talks

FOR COUPLES

In the movie Ground Hog Day, *Bill Murray kept waking up only to repeat the same day over and over again. What recent day would you not want to repeat?*

In the movie Ground Hog Day, *Bill Murray kept waking*

up only to repeat the same day over and over again.

What recent day would you not want to repeat?

What old photograph of yourself makes you really laugh or cringe in embarrassment?

Love Talks
FOR COUPLES

What old photograph of yourself makes you

really laugh or cringe in embarrassment?

Recall something about exchanging valentines

when you were in elementary school.

Recall something about exchanging valentines

when you were in elementary school.

Love Talks

FOR COUPLES

Congratulations! Your boss just gave everyone

a spring break. Where do you want to go?

Love Talks
FOR COUPLES

*Congratulations! Your boss just gave everyone
a spring break. Where do you want to go?*

What is something that occurred this past year that you are especially thankful for?

Love Talks
FOR COUPLES

— QUESTION 101 —

What is something that occurred this past year

that you are especially thankful for?

Love Talks

FOR COUPLES